welcome to

Twinkle Pants

PUFFIN BOOKS

People call me Twinkle Pants
Cos if I had my way
I'd wear all sorts of sparkly stuff
To make me shine all day!

Check me in my absolutely MOST favourite pants!!

When my loud alarm clock rings
I really can't stop yawning
I wish that I could turn it off
And stay in bed all morning!

My bedroom's full of photos
And posters on the walls
I also just love fairy lights
And groovy glitter balls!

I open up my wardrobe
And there's loads of clothes in there
So how come I can never find
A single thing to wear?

I've got a lot of ringtones
And graphics for my screen
And some really funky fascias
Cos I'm a mobile queen!

There's nothing I like better
Than going out with pals
Looking out for groovy clothes
In shiny shopping malls!

Me and my best buddy
Love slobbing in our jeans
Flicking through a massive pile
Of funky magazines!

We go into the bathroom
With our bulging make-up cases
And spend an hour or maybe two
Just making up our faces!

If the saying's true
That what you wear is what you are
My Twinkle Pants will make me
A shiny superstar!

PUFFIN BOOKS

Published by the Penguin Group

Penguin Books Ltd, 80 Strand, London WC2R 0RL, England

Penguin Putnam Inc., 375 Hudson Street, New York, New York 10014, USA

Penguin Books Australia Ltd, 250 Camberwell Road, Camberwell, Victoria 3124, Australia

Penguin Books Canada Ltd, 10 Alcorn Avenue, Toronto, Ontario, Canada M4V 3B2

Penguin Books India (P) Ltd, 11 Community Centre, Panchsheel Park, New Delhi - 110 017, India

Penguin Books (NZ) Ltd, Cnr Rosedale and Airborne Roads, Albany, Auckland, New Zealand

Penguin Books (South Africa) (Pty) Ltd, 24 Sturdee Avenue, Rosebank 2196, South Africa

Penguin Books Ltd, Registered Offices: 80 Strand, London WC2R 0RL, England

www.penguin.com

First published 2003

1

© Giles Andreae

Set in magicpants

Manufactured in Malaysia

British Library Cataloguing in Publication Data
A CIP catalogue record for this book is available from the British Library

ISBN 0-141-31554-7